D1212765

Panorama-Books: SALZBURG

With thirty colour plates

WOLFGANG KUDRNOFSKY

SALZBURG

AND SURROUNDINGS

Translated by G. A. Colville

LIBRARY
SEMINOLE JR. COLLEGE

Rec.   JAN 1 9 1970

SANFORD, FLORIDA

VIENNA

WILHELM ANDERMANN VERLAG

Wrapper and cover designed by Gerhard M. Hotop.

U. S. Distributors

FRENCH & EUROPEAN PUBLICATIONS Inc.

Rockefeller Center, New York, N. Y.

© 1961 by Wilhelm Andermann, Vienna. All rights reserved by the publisher.

Printed in Austria.

Exactly in the centre of Austria lies the Salzkammergut, a district which stretches over three regional provinces. Everything that Europe has to offer that is beautiful and worth seeing seems here to be combined. Times and spaces lie closely side by side, the contrasts making good neighbours. While the chills of the Ice Age blow over the mountain glaciers, a friendly, warmer air-stream sighs over the summery lakes, filling the boat-sails. In the light of day the people go about their manifold tasks, while under the earth, in eternal night, wait the salt minerals to be brought up into the light of the upper world.

Salt and sun are the two elements of life in the Salzkammergut. In salt and sun lie the power of life: In sale et sole omnia consistunt.

The region formed by the Hallstättersee and Aussee districts got its name from the salt present in great quantities in their mountains. Already, Celts, Romans and Germans dug here after salt. Indeed, in prehistoric times an individual culture had developed around the mining of it — the "Hallstätter Culture" — determined following rich finds.

Then, at the beginning of our last thousand years, the Princes then living thereabouts were equally clever at knowing how to make the wealth of the country theirs. The profits from the working of the salt flowed into the princely treasure chambers, and the name of "Ischlland" became thereby changed into "Salzkammergut" — as the region is still called. Until 1786, up to the reign of the Emperor Josef II, the Salzkammergut enjoyed many privileges not possessed by the other Austrian provinces: thus it had its own administration, at the head of which stood a "Salt Office Man".

This official was not only the supreme chief of the salt installations — a very much sought after office — but he also exercised the duties of judge and police.

Then, for hundreds — perhaps thousands — of years the Salzkammergut was known and famed for the salt lying buried in its hills. Then, in the eighteenth century, an interest started to be taken in the countryside itself also. It became the fashion to follow the call of the Swiss Frenchman Jean Jaques Rousseau to go out in search of nature. And when, in 1809, the doctor and naturalist Josef August Schultes praised the natural beauty of this countryside in his "Travels through Upper Austria", soon the first summer visitors came into the Salzkammergut. The townspeople, unused to nature, were seized with admiration for the romanticism and the harmony of mountain, valley and lake. Soon the country was being called the "Austrian Switzerland", and, finally, when the Austrian ruling house made Bad Ischl its summer residence, it became the focal point for tourists. Such an event was important for the people of those times. It was preceded by a discovery, still of significance, of the Viennese doctor Dr. Wirer. He came to Ischl in 1821 and soon discovered that the salt solution from which the salt is won through evaporation, and in which still other important minerals are exposed, is of a healing strength similar to that of natural seawater. To make this operation accessible to large numbers of people, Dr. Wirer erected a saltwater bath in Bad Ischl. Other places in the neighbourhood followed his example, and today the Salzkammergut possesses numerous large baths almost all of which are fed from their own springs. Solely Bad Gmunden draws its saltwater from Ischl.

Thus it was that the Austrian Emperors combined the beautiful with the practical, relishing at one and the same time the beauty of the landscape around their summer residence and the benefits accruing from curative possibilities. Many thousands of visitors still follow their example.

The Salzkammergut is some two-and-a-half thousand square kilometres in extent. Of this, three-quarters is part of the federal province of Upper

Austria, the rest being divided up between Salzburg and Styria. Most of the lakes lie in Upper Austria, including the two largest, the Attersee and the Traunsee. In Salzburg and Styria the lakes are relatively fewer and smaller. Since the term "Salzkammergut" is not precisely outlined and "Salt and Sun" are not sufficient, a simple rule of thumb has been evolved to define it. Salzkammergut consists of the whole of the territory where there is a lake not more than twenty kilometres away. Because Upper Austria has the most lakes, the greater portion of the Salzkammergut belongs to it.

Where the shadows of the great chains of mountains reach out into the northern plateau lie the most extensive lakes. Of these, the Attersee, or Kammersee, twenty kilometres long and an average of three kilometres wide, is the most important. It represents the link between the region's two geographical extremities. Its northern end lies in the flat Alpine foreland, while the southern tip reaches into the higher spurs of the Alps.

To these spurs belongs the steep, almost 1800-metre-high Schafberg, a natural observation-point, giving wonderful views over the spreading countryside. Whoever has made a journey by the rack railway over the rapidly ascending face of this mountain will scarcely ever forget the beauty of the changing picture which is offered him. From St. Wolfgang the railway follows in a north-westerly direction over the steepest slopes. At first the surrounding chains of mountains preclude any extensive prospect, but slowly the Wolfgangsee, lying in the valley basin, displays the whole of its banks the further one draws away. It is as if it is placing itself on exhibition and would always loom larger — an unforgettable picture. Then there quickly comes another surprise. Under the always more magnificently vaulting dome of heaven, the mountains and hills fringing the lake seem to become pressed together and sink down, and behind their by now almost vanished and smaller silhouette there suddenly appear in the far distance sun-drenched glaciers from the Ice Age, gaining in breath and plenitude. The beauty of the landscape just passed through is forgotten. It is as if the giants of the primeval age were exhibiting themselves as a Fata Morgana, with the mighty Dachstein standing massively over all.

Other mountains group themselves about the far-off mighty peak. To the west, the massif of the Hohen Zinken has suddenly appeared. To the east, the Tote Gebirge is visible. And soon one is surrounded by a completely different panorama, as if the sky were pressing nearer.

A short while later, however, this grandiose impression, too, is excelled. The railway has reached the summit. A few metres remain to be covered on foot, to the look-out plateau in front of the mountain-hotel, and then one stands on the highest tip of the Schafberg. And now for the visitor the Salzkammergut spreads itself out many hundreds of metres below. Screened by a light-bluish haze from the radiant gold of the sun, the celestially-coloured lakes lie embedded in the midst of graceful hill-country, fragments of a great mirror under which millions of years ago there lay concealed, in silent obscurity, the flourishing, blossoming land of today. In the distance, the wreath of hills and mountains, now closely one with the horizon, encloses on every side the lake-plateau lying there at our feet. If we had any desire to go on farther we should soon realise that over the yonder chain of mountains still stretched this wonderful landscape, but then the individual impressions in the complete picture would dissolve away. Let us, therefore, be satisfied with the little, grandiose poem that the Creator has written round the Schafberg and find enjoyment in gazing at it again and again.

Apart from the great Attersee, two other lakes give directly on the Schafberg — to the west the Mondsee, and to the south the Wolfgang- or Abersee. While Wolfgang and Mondsee — of more or less equal size — are already part of the secondary mountain country, the Attersee, just as its somewhat more distantly-lying eastern neighbour the Traunsee, is a valley lake. All these lakes are straggling and narrow, and their position is determined by geographical requirements. The northern-lying lakes follow a north-south direction, the others the self-willed course of the mountain valleys.

On St. Wolfgangsee, the left half of which lies in the province of Salzburg, is the marketing-place of St. Wolfgang. For its name it has to thank St. Wolfgang, who lived here for five years — from 972 to 977. For this reason the place is still a resort of pilgrims, although many visitors come only because of the superbly carved altar of Michael

Pacher. It has stood in St. Wolfgang's Gothic church for nearly five hundred years. This altar is the principal work of the famous artist. His wood-carved figures represent the consecration by the Lord of the World of the crowned Queen of Heaven. Inside, the panelled picture shows the story of the Virgin Mary. When the altar is once closed there is seen the miracle of Christ and, when the wings are entirely closed, the legend of St. Wolfgang.

Of rather more recent date and more of local interest are the two objects worth seeing that the village and summer holiday resort of St. Gilgen have offer. St. Gilgen, which lies at the opposite end of the lake, in the Salzburg province, commemorates another Wolfgang. Though no saint, he would certainly still be equally beloved in Heaven. He was Wolfgang Amadeus Mozart. In St. Gilgen, which is some twenty-five kilometres from the Mozart town of Salzburg. Mozart's mother was born in a little house close to the lakeside. A wonderfully beautiful little fountain, erected in front of the local village council's offices, testifies to the memory of her son.

Only some five kilometres north of the Wolfgangsee and parallel to it lies the Mondsee, into the waters of which, on the southern shore, fall the slopes of the Schafberg, with its spurs the Höllkar and the wildly ragged Drachenwand. The road, like all those by the Salzkammergut lakes, follows the lake bank as closely as the terrain permits and, indeed, at several places has to pass through the steeply-ascending wall of rock.

Mondsee — not only the place of the same name but also the other territory round the lake — was inhabited by people from very early times. Indeed, in 1871 a lake-dwelling dating from the Early Stone Age was discovered here. At the same point in prehistoric times as men lived here, the settlements of the "Hallstatt Culture" were also set up. The village of Mondsee is well-known through its Benedictine monastery, endowed in 784 but secularised in 1787, since when it has served as a castle.

Just as Mondsee's waters flow via the little river Ache into the Attersee, so does the same-named Zeller Ache perform the same duties at the other end. It carries the water off from the Zellersee, the most northerly-situated of the Upper Austrian lakes, into the Mondsee.

In the province of Salzburg lies still more to the north a group of smaller lakes. With them, the Salzkammergut comes to an end in this direction. They are the Wallersee, the Grabensee, and the two Mattseen, the Upper and the Lower Trummer lakes. Between the last two named lies the village of Mattsee, with its religious establishment, founded in 777 by the Bavarian Duke Tasillo. The Gothic church, with its rich baroque embellishments, and the religious foundation, with its fine cloisters, are truly worth visiting. Through the little Grabensee, which lies north-west of the two Matt lakes, the Mattig flows in a northerly direction, to join the Inn near Braunau.

All the lakes mentioned up to now form, with their great chains, one whole. Lying in part closely together, they are also directly connected with one another through the Ache or smaller streams. This western group of lakes lies opposite the numerically much fewer lakes in the east of the region. These are more widely separated from each other but they are related by a special link that underlines their interdependence. This link is the 180-kilometre-long Traun, which rises in the Styrian part of the Salzkammergut, its waters coming from the Ödensee Traun, the Altaussee Traun — which drains the lake of the name — and the Grundlsee. These three streams unite with the Traun itself near Bad Aussee and the river then flows on the Hallstättersee through the narrow Koppenvalley between the Zinkenkogel and the Sarstein. On its long way through the Salzkammergut, the Traun passes Goisern and Ischl. Near Ebensee it flows into the Traunsee, which is sometimes called the Gmundnersee. At Gmunden it leaves the Salzkammergut once more, to flow directly through the Alpine foreland towards the Danube, in which it finally empties itself.

The course of the Traun extends, therefore, from the southern boundary of the Salzkammergut up to, and beyond, its northernmost limit. Since on this journey it flows through the heart of the region, Bad Ischl, it might almost be said to be a life's artery. It was indeed that for a long time for the inhabitants of the district. As there were no wide roads or speedy railways for transport purposes, the salt that was extracted from the Hallstatt, Ischl and Ebensee mines was brought northwards in great barges on the Traun for further transport by the Danube.

And without the Traun the whole of this eastern lake-country would be unthinkable. Lovely as it is from the landscape point of view, this section would really be without a "heart".

So at the back of the Toten mountains, where Upper Austria ends and Styria begins, lies the source of the Traun. The climate hereabouts is relatively rawer than in the more north-lying flatland. The district's two lakes — the Grundlsee and the Altausseersee — are colder than their northern brothers, since they lie more strongly in the shadow of the mountain range, the spurs of which come down to the edges of the lakes. Where the three little streams unite with the Traun lies Bad Aussee, the centre of the Styrian part of the Salzkammergut. As a well-known spa, it offers the ailing manifold possibilities for convalescence and recreation. Apart from the tourist traffic, the salt works are still most important for the local people. The things most worth seeing in Bad Aussee are the 15th-century Salt Office buildings, the Late Gothic parish church and the Gothic wing-altar in the Spital's church.

Below Bad Aussee the bed of the Traun slopes southerly, to turn finally north again below the Hallstättersee. This winding detour takes the Traun to the Krippenstein, at the foot of which are to be found the famous Dachstein caverns. Its summit can also be reached by means of the newly-constructed cable railway.

On the western bank of the gloomy, cold Hallstättersee and on the wooded slopes of the Hallstättersee salt-mountain lies the marketing-place of Hallstatt with its two celebrated churches. The Catholic one contains a 15th-century wing-altar. Belonging to the school of Michael Pacher, it was worked on for ten years and is very like the St. Wolfgang altar. Hallstatt's age-old salt-mine, which still exists, was certainly already being worked in prehistoric times. Finds of the remains of planking and wooden and bronze implements lead to the conclusion that the mine dates from the Bronze Age.

Near Hallstatt, on the "High Valley" at Rudolf's Tower, a great prehistoric burial-ground, with twenty-five hundred graves of people who had been cremated or otherwise, and bronze and iron implements that had been buried with them were uncovered during the second half of the last century. These finds caused the historical cultural experts to speak of a particular cultural circle, the "Hallstatt Culture".

We have the Hallstättersee at the spot where the Traun flows onwards and wander along the Traun valley further towards the north. Thereby we come to Bad Goisern, the bromine and iodine bathing resort with its beautiful old houses. Only ten kilometres farther on, and we now stand in the very centre of Salzkammergut's heart, Bad Ischl.

Bad Ischl, health resort and former Imperial summer residence, was declared a market-town in 1466 and became officially a town in 1941. The centre of spa activity is the Kurhaus, built by Clemens Holzmeister.

Bad Ischl was until recently, too, the terminus of the Salzkammergut railway running from Salzburg through the region, taking travellers to the most important picturesque stations of the eastern part of the Salzkammergut.

Here the Traun is wider. It absorbs the water of the Ischl and then flows on in a north-easterly direction towards the second largest of the Salzkammergut lakes, the Traunsee.

The Traunsee, or Gmundnersee as it is sometimes called, stretches from Ebensee in the south to Gmunden in the north. Ebensee is the valley-station of the Feuerkogel railway. It is a little summer holiday resort, located exactly where the Traun flows into the lake. The Feuerkogel, some 1600 metres high, is an offshoot of the Höllengebirge and attracts many visitors in winter because of the numerous ski excursions possible from here. Ebensee is the last place on the Traun where the inhabitants mostly live from the salt industry. With the great salt-works here, the range of salt-extracting places along the river comes to an end.

Along the west bank of the Traunsee the roads winds on through the village of Traunkirchen, with a celebrated parish church, and branches off towards Gmunden. The Gothic church of Altmünster and Castle Orth, built in the Traunsee itself, are the first visible heralds of this most northerly town in the Salzkammergut. Its extensive grounds and gardens and its lively spa business remind one a little of the garden-town of Ischl. But already in the Gothic era, from which period dates the Town Hall,

Salzburg, Blick vom Mönchsberg auf die Festung
Salzburg, View of the Fortress from the Mönchsberg
Salzbourg, la forteresse vue du Mönchsberg

Salzburg, Residenzplatz
Salzburg, Residenz Square
Salzbourg, la place de la Résidence

Salzburg, Dreifaltigkeitskirche
Salzburg, Church of the Trinity
Salzbourg, Eglise de la Trinité

Schloß Fuschl
Castle Fuschl
Le château
de Fuschl

Kreuz im Mondsee
Cross in the Mondsee
Croix au Mondsee

Mondsee

Schafbergalpe

*Blick vom Schafberg
auf den Mondsee*
*View from the
Schafberg*
*Le Mondsee vu du
Schafberg*

Der Pacher-Altar in St. Wolfgang

Pacher Altar at St. Wolfgang

L'autel Pacher de St. Wolfgang

Barockkirche in Strobl
Baroque Church in Strobl
Eglise baroque à Strobl

Bad Ischl, Blick von der Lehár-Villa
Bad Ischl, seen from the Lehár-Villa
Bad Ischl, vu du Lehár-Villa

Die Kaiser-Villa in Bad Ischl
Imperial Villa at Bad Ischl
La villa de l'empereur à Bad Ischl

Bad Goisern

Hallstatt

Gosausee

Eishöhle im Dachstein
Ice Cavern in the
Dachstein Mountains
Caverne de glace dans
les Monts Dachstein

Grundlsee

Schloß Orth im Traunsee
Castle Orth in the Traunsee
Le château d'Orth au Traunsee

Gmunden am Traunsee

Langbathsee

Kreuz in der Tra
Cross in the Tra
Croix sur la rivière Tra

*Fischer-Kanzel in
Traunkirchen*

*Chancel in
Traunkirchen Church
with Motives of
Christ and the
Fishermen*

*La chaire de la Pêche
miraculeuse à
Traunkirchen*

Attersee

the parish church and the house of the old town, give it more weight than the other town today has, and the milder and warmer climate of the Alpine foreland is pleasanter here.

So on flows the Traun. Arriving at Lambach, the northern gateway to the Salzkammergut, it finally leaves the lovely land. The great Danube is waiting to receive its waters, waters that trickle out of the earth in the shade of the Styrian mountains, to flow on through the uniquely lovely countryside, past centuries-old places of culture. The quick little waves wander still further, leaving behind them their homeland's times and spaces.

In the Salzkammergut countryside it is the natural arrangement that is responsible for the magical, precise harmony. Near-by Salzburg, on the other hand, has human hands to thank for its wonderful composition. Here the building development has placidly expanded between the Mönchsberg and the Kapuzinerberg hills, following the line of the river Salzach, but it has, all the same, left room enough for the natural to be combined with the practical in beauty.

The origin of this town, which today has over one hundred thousand inhabitants, lies somewhere in the subconscious darkness of the prehistoric past. For its present name it has, of course, to thank the valuable substance of the mountain-salt. Only on the Rainberg, on the south-west boundary of the town of today, are some traces to be found of Salzburg's long-ago.

So far as historical authenticity is concerned, Salzburg introduces itself for the first time as Juvavum. Unlike most other Roman settlements in northern regions, Juvavum was no military encampment but the seat of administration for the whole district. As its prehistoric predecessor, this settlement was located on the left bank of the Salzach, though thick on the bank and flanked by the steep, protective Mönchsberg. The right bank belonged to the dead. Around the present Mirabell Square, burial grounds were laid out as eternal resting-places for those Roman administrators who had died in foreign parts.

Juvavum grew rapidly. About 200 A. D. was the town's period of efflorescence. Soon afterwards, somewhere about the year 470, it was swept away again through the stresses of racial migration. A Christian basilica had once been erected before its walls, so the contemporary chronicles of St. Severinus report.

Two hundred years later, in the seventh century, St. Rupert founded the religious establishment of St. Peter, and St. Erentrudis the Benedictine monastery of the Nonnberg foundation. Both buildings have been preserved to this day even though subsequently they were naturally repeatedly altered and extended. They represent, therefore, the nuclei of the municipal organism that, from then on, thrived continually and was hardly ever menaced during the following centuries.

Then, in 774, shortly after, Salzburg received a symbol — the Cathedral. This was not the House of God which is today indivisibly connected in the mind of the visitor with the image of Salzburg, since the original Cathedral was burnt down soon after it was completed and subsequent buildings suffered the same fate several times. Alone the building reconstructed afresh in the twelfth century has been preserved for modern times. The ground in front of the Cathedral is at present being excavated in order to expose the foundation of the earlier buildings.

With the erection in the eighth century of the first Cathedral, the development of Salzburg as a burgher-town started. For the time being, however, its boundaries did not extend beyond those of the former Roman settlement of Juvavum. Nevertheless, in 1077 the town did spread beyond its existing boundaries. On the heights of the Mönchsberg was built the fortress of Hohensalzburg. Now, after the great church, Salzburg had also received its citadel. Therewith the town of Salzburg felt itself part of the international world and began slowly to expand, first along the left bank of the Salzach, upstream as well as downstream. In the twelfth century it at last spilled over to the right bank of the river — the former Roman burial preserve. There, where the only bridge of the Salzburg of those times crossed the river, a little settlement started being built about a church that in the interim has vanished. The former Town Hall also stood near this bridge. As time went on, the district upstream continued to be built on until at length the final stage was reached between the Franz-Josef and Rudolf quays.

In this — for Salzburg — so important a century, when many structural alterations were undertaken, the town received for the first time a town wall which put a check for the time being to further extension. It was artificially extended where the natural protective wall of Salzburg's own Mönchsberg, Festungsberg and Kapuzinerberg seemed not strong enough. The town wall then continued to the declivity of the Nonnberg along the Salzach as far as the Bürgerspital which was founded in the fourteenth century. On the other bank it continued, in line with the present Königsgasse and Ledergasse, as far as the beginning of the Kapuzinerberg at the spot where the former eastern gate stood. The first great alteration to this protective girdle was undertaken in the fifteenth century, when the further extension of that part on the right bank of the Salzach was put in hand. The second and last great change took place during the Thirty Years' War under the supervision of the Cathedral's architect Satino Solari at the command of the then Salzburg Archbishop Paris Lodron who wished to extend the town beyond its existing boundaries. The great protective structure is still preserved only where, because of the difficult terrain conditions on the Mönchsberg and the Kapuzinerberg, no new buildings could be created. In the town of Salzburg itself there are only a few disconnected remains extant. The greatest relic of the mediaeval arrangement is to be found at the western boundary of the Mirabell Gardens which likewise date from those times.

Shortly before the erection of the Lodron fortifications, far-reaching alterations to the town's arrangement itself were put in hand by the

Prince Bishop Wolf Dietrich von Raithenau. The Cathedral cemetery on the site of the present Residenz Square was done away with and the Sebastian cemetery created in its stead on the edge of the right part of the town. Some hundred buildings were demolished in order to make room for four great squares about the Cathedral. The "Gries" was established as a residential area and new streets were opened up. The Cathedral, which was partly burnt down, was pompously rebuilt after the fashion of the time. For most of the work the Bishop called in the assistance of architects of the Italian school. The initiator of all these municipal structural alterations, the afore-mentioned Prince Bishop von Raithenau, was also the responsible builder of the celebrated Mirabell seat on the right bank of the Salzach. What he created, one of his successors, the Archbishop Lodron, was able to render secure by the erection of his extended girdle of fortifications.

In the coming years the grandiose new profile of the town was, however, to lose its significance very quickly. The squares which had been exposed were soon again built on, this time, however, with non-ecclesiastical structures. Then, beside the Lodron palaces and the Collegiate Church the University was built, and when really no more place was to be found for a big structure there was erected on the open spots at least a fountain. Building space was so limited that soon in the thickly-populated quarters of the town the houses had to go up to as many as five storeys high. These houses still stand. They impress through their narrow, elegantly smooth façades, the single enlivenment of which consists incidentally of a one-piece framework round small windows.

Meanwhile in the centre of the burgher town of Salzburg another Salzburg has grown up. This was the town of the ecclesiastical and worldly princes — the representative and monumental Salzburg composed of wonderful buildings and art treasures which remains imprisoned in the memory of the visitor for ever. That other Salzburg, however, middle-class and homely, though providing us with less material for our imagination and remembrance, all the more conveys to us something of the former atmosphere. In this lies Salzburg's history; in that other, its poetry.

Who gazes over Salzburg from one of the town's three mountains realises at once the difference. Towering and conspicuous are the churches, the palaces, the stretches of gardens. And, forming the link, are the rows of roofs of differing heights and the channels of lanes in front of the houses with, in between, great square-shaped court-openings. The unique picture of Salzburg derives primarily from this aspect.

The roofs of the Salzburg houses are often likened to those of the Italian Renaissance. As a comparison it may well be accepted, although there were actually such roofs in Salzburg before the Italian Renaissance. They owe their form not to any feeling for style but to a practical need. The roof-culvert, which is covered over by a tiny wall and so is invisible from the street, is made up of low, saddle-shaped roofs set one behind the other. Among them are the culverts, which have the important task of chanelling away, before the streets get over-flooded, the rainwater that so frequently open outs upon Salzburg in something like cloudbursts.

In addition to the types of roofs, the house façades have been preserved in the original parts of Salzburg. The dwellings behind them are small and congested, and the court-yards, often necessary because of the depth of the houses, are picturesque and jolly arcades, able to express the sentiment of the time: "My home is my castle".

Naturally the lanes in between these houses have not become wider in the meantime — a very uncomfortable fact for many car-drivers. It is, however, a blessing so far as the picturesque aspect of the old town is concerned, for many streets there remain undisturbed by the mass of today's traffic. The town would not be half so beautiful if automobiles could dash along streets where the pedestrian scarcely finds a place. The new time is commonplace enough for it to be a good thing that here a little bit of the Middle Ages remains alive. The distances, too, are so small that anybody can travel them on foot. Salzburg demonstrates its centuries-old will of its own by standing aloof from doubtful "advances" in disturbing the lay-out of the town. This will of its own often prevented it in the course of history from becoming a sacrifice of the times. For almost a thousand years it was the seat of independent Princes, the Archbishops of Salzburg. While during the Thirty Years' War the country outside was devastated and the people annihilated, behind the walls of Salzburg its symbol, the Cathedral, was happily completed, the Town

Hall, the asylum of public life, enlarged, the university founded, the fortification walls at last strengthened. And all with the right idea not to permit Salzburg to be disturbed in the future through the wrangling of warlike neighbours.

Its evolution has rewarded this policy. Today, Salzburg is a town whose opulence in treasures of the past is both admired and sought after. In 1930 it possessed a quarter of a million people, about five times the number of the original inhabitants. And where else is there such a town which so forcefully displays its attraction?

TO THE PICTURES

Salzburg, view of the Fortress from the Mönchsberg

Salzburg's characteristic feature, the Hohensalzburg fortress, can be seen from far away yet it lies only some 130 metres above the level of the town. From it, however, it is possible to get a far-reaching prospect over Salzburg, particularly if one climbs the Tower of Justice, another 40 metres high. Built in 1077, during the period of the struggle between Emperor and Pope, the citadel was given its present structural form between 1465 and 1519. In 1861 it ceased to be a fortress and to-day serves only as a museum and to give visitors an impression of former building styles.

The individual parts of the citadel, its towers and protective archways, are soberly and massively carried out. The inner rooms alone are fitted out in the style of later times, exhibiting typical elements of these. Thus the Prince's Room is filled with examples of Gothic art, including a Late Gothic tiled stove dating from the year 1501 — an especially valuable piece and, indeed, the most beautiful now remaining of that period. The fortress's little George Church is also wholly in the Gothic style.

Residenz Square in Salzburg

Throughout many centuries the Residenz was the intellectual centre of Salzburg. To it in 1120 came the Archbishop of St. Peter's, therewith raising the Residenz to the permanent seat of the Court. Since the Salzburg Bishops were also independent Princes, the Residenz housed at one and the same time the keeper of the spiritual and terrestrial orders in his person.

Residenz Square is surrounded by the adjoining Cathedral, the Bell Tower (picture, right) and the Michael's Church (left). The Residenz Fountain in the middle of the square was built during 1656 to 1661. It is the greatest baroque fountain in Central Europe. Its diameter is 15 metres.

Church of the Trinity in Salzburg

This church lies in the newer part of the town. It is the work of the celebrated baroque master-builder Johann von Erlach and was built between 1694 and 1702. In 1818 parts of the church were destroyed by fire. The reconstruction is not, however, as successful as was the original building.

Thus, for example, the dome now recedes too much in the background compared with the two towers. Nevertheless, the church still belongs to Salzburg's baroque treasures.

Fuschl

If you come into the Salzkammergut from Salzburg, the Fuschlsee is the first of the many lakes to greet you there. There you can visit Castle Fuschl and the Wartenfels ruins and get "the Mozart view".

It is no longer known when Castle Fuschl was built and completed. Originally it was an archbishop's hunting castle. Since 1865, however, it has been in private ownership. It contains some interesting Late Gothic and baroque pictures.

The Mondsee. Cross in the Mondsee

Eight years ago the Mondsee revealed something of its earliest past. Lake-dwellings were built on the shores of the lake during the Bronze Age and it was possible to identify their remains. They are ascribed to a

unique "Mondsee Cultural Group".
The cross in the foreground dates from
a later period.

The Mondsee Market-town

At the northern end of the Mondsee
lies the summer holiday resort of the
same name. It is famed for its religious establishment, which was founded in 784 by the Benedictines, whom
it served until it became a secular
castle in 1787.

The place of Mondsee was first mentioned in 748 as an endowment of the
Benedictine monastery. This former
religious establishment shows a mix-
ture of Late Gothic and baroque
styles. While the building of the present parish church, which was for-
merly the collegiate church, follows
the plan of Late Gothic stepped churches, its interior lay-out, above all the
altars, is modelled on baroque and
later styles.

Schafbergalpe

The Schafberg railway, which starts
at St. Wolfgang, halts shortly before
its terminus, at the "Schafbergalpe" —
a mountain hut providing shelter. Since
the peak of the Schafberg shuts out
part of the view, the prospect from
here over the mountainous part of the
Salzkammergut is limited. In the picture you can see the Hochkönig behind
the Schafbergalpe.

View from the Schafberg

One has the grandest of all views
over the Salzkammergut from the
Schafberg. It is encircled by three of
the most beautiful of the Salzkammergut lakes and before it rise the
southern mountain massifs — a landscape for the similar many-sidedness
of which one has to search about. Our
picture shows the Mondsee as seen
from the Schafberg.

St. Gilgen

St. Gilgen lies on the north-west tip
of the Wolfgangsee. Wolfgang Amadeus Mozart's mother was born in a
little house here.

St. Gilgen, which has a particularly
fine position on the shores of the lake,

is much favoured as a summer holiday resort. The parish church in the middle of the village shows strong Romanesque influences although it was mentioned for the first time in the fourteenth century. Its tower dates from the Late Gothic period and shows the double-arched windows characteristic of it. In the interior is an altar painting by the rococo painter Lorenzoni.

White Horse on Wolfgangsee

Besides its historical attractions, St. Wolfgang exhibits also something very much of later times. This is the "White Horse" on Wolfgangsee, known throughout the world from the operetta of the same name.

Pacher Altar at St. Wolfgang

In 1471, the most celebrated Gothic painter and sculptor, Michael Pacher, entered into a contract with the St. Wolfgang parish authorities. Pacher was to carve and paint a wing-altar for the church — the celebrated pilgrims' church which, it is alleged, was built in the tenth century by St. Wolfgang himself. The work was completed ten years later. With it, Pacher created his most beautiful piece and at the same time the most famous carving of his era.

Strobl

Strobl lies on the east side of the Wolfgangsee, opposite St. Gilgen. As all places on this lake, it serves chiefly as a summer holiday resort. The lovely baroque church dates from the year 1758 and was built by Kassian Singer. Inside, in addition to a painting by Benedikt Werkstätter there is a work by the baroque artist P. A. Lorenzoni, the painter of the St. Gilgen altar picture.

Lehár Villa at Ischl

Franz Lehár, who from being an orchestral violinist and conductor of a military band became the most successful Viennese operetta composer, spent a large part of his life in Ischl where he had a villa built, the exuberant ostentation of which can be seen by the visitor today. Lehár died in 1948.

Imperial Villa at Bad Ischl

When the Emperor Franz Josef took up his summer residence in Ischl in the middle of the last century, he made the place at the same time the much desired summer holiday resort for the high aristocratic and financial world of Old Austria. Many artists also came regularly for recuperation to Ischl, among them the celebrated Johann Nestroy who after the middle of the century lived permanently in Ischl.

Goisern

North of the Hallstättersee, on the road to Ischl, lies Goisern, summer holiday resort and winter-sport place, celebrated through its rare iodine and bromine sulphur wells.

The inhabitants of the district round the Hallstättersee suffered greatly from the prevailing tension during the Counter Reformation. In many places in the district there was also a Pro-

testant parish church side by side with the otherwise general Catholic one. Such was the case at Goisern, just as at Hallstatt itself.

Hallstatt

Hugging the shores of its lake lies picturesque Hallstatt. Mostly it is hidden in the shade of its mountains which here slant steeply into the water. A slim, towering pillar shows a long way off — the tower of the Catholic parish church. Inside is an altar reminiscent in many ways of Pacher's at St. Wolfgang.

Hallstatt is also known for its saltmines which were worked in earlier days exactly as they are today.

Hallstatt Museum

The little town has a small museum in which there is collected and exhibited much to do with Hallstatt's natural and cultural history. Included is the historic old drainage system from the Hallstatt salt-mine works which has, of course, been supplanted by a modern installation.

Gosausee

From the road along the banks of the Hallstättersee leads a branch to Gosausee, which lies some 20 kilometres distant. At the very beginning of the lake there presents itself to the observer the magnificent panorama of the Dachstein, some 3.000 metres high, with its many peaks (Hoher Dachstein, Torstein, Grimming, "Bishop's Mitre", etc.) and its six glaciers.

Ice Cavern in the Dachstein Mountains

This ice cavern was discovered and and rendered accessible during the last century. The two caverns were made suitable for visitors for the first time recently. They are the Giant Ice Cavern, with grandiose natural ice formations, and the Mammoth Cavern, whose far-reaching tube-shaped tunnel was formed by a subterranean river.

Altaussee

This place belongs already to the Styrian part of the Salzkammergut. Its surroundings are cool, raw and mountainy. In spite of this, it is a favoured goal for summer tourists. The two most notable features of the Altaussee's lakeside panorama are the Tote Gebirge and the steeply towering Trisselwand.

Mitterndorf

Mitterndorf, on the southern boundary of the Salzkammergut, is the meeting-place for mountain lovers and ramblers. It lies in the Styrian valley of the Salzkammergut at the foot of the Tote Gebirge, embedded in the valley between Rostelstein, Lawinenstein and the twenty-five-hundred-metre-high Grimming.

The beautiful parish church of St. Margaret dates from the 14th century.

Grundlsee

Three kilometres east of Bad Aussee lies the Grundlsee, 414 hectares in extent, in which many fish abound. It belongs to the Styrian part of the Salzkammergut and is one of the lakes whose waters flow into the river Traun.

Castle Orth

If you come from the south along the lakeside road of the Traunsee towards Gmunden, Castle Orth shows you your goal from far away. A wooden bridge leads from the castle on the mainland to the lake-castle, built in the 17th century. The former owner of Castle Orth was the Archduke Johann Salvator (Johann Orth) who later vanished.

Gmunden

Gmunden on the Traunsee is the most northerly town in the Salzkammergut. Although it has no wells of its own, it is however, renowned as a health resort. Its health-giving waters come from Bad Ischl, thirty kilometres away. Its old houses, Town Hall, Late Gothic church and, not least, its marvellous view over the Traunsee shores make it particularly distinguished.

Langbathsee

Westwards from Ebensee a little road leads through the Langbath valley to the two small, rather lonely, lakes of the district. The Langbath valley itself lies at the northern foot of the Feuerkogel.

Traunkirchen

Traunkirchen lies picturesquely between Ebensee and Gmunden on the west bank of the Traunsee on a rock jutting far out into the lake. The Johannes Chapel, dating from the seventeenth century, with the walled-in Römerstein, is visible from far out in the lake.

Chancel in Traunkirchen

In the parish church of Traunkirchen is to be seen a richly-decorated wood-carved chancel dating from 1753. It illustrates, in the form of a ship with statues of the Apostles, the story of the miracle of the fishes. The church itself is a former convent church. It was completely rebuilt after a fire in 1632.

man had erected in memory of his beloved wife.

Cross in the Traun

The Traun rises in the Aussee district and flows in a northerly direction through the whole of the Salzkammergut. Below Bad Ischl, where it turns north-east, there stands in the middle of the river a cross which a

Attersee

This lake, which is also called Kammersee, is the largest lake in the Salzkammergut. It stretches up into the northern flat-lands. It is 170 metres deep. The whole district round the lake is called Attergau.